Love, Loss, and Remembrance:

A Poetry Anthology

By Selma Ruth Wolkow

To Mary Ellen
with Best Wishes

May 2014

ISBN 978-1-312-28743-3
90000
9 781312 287433

11/21/15

A Special Day in July

(Cover Photo)

Kids, come downstairs into the sun and I'll take a picture
Of you both.
This was 1945, just the old black box camera
Available then.

It was late July.
The "Boy" I had met 14 months before,
And had corresponded with
While he had been fighting in Europe
Was at last,
Home on a 30 day furlough
Before heading off to fight in Japan.
But two fiery blasts saved his life,
And so many, many others, from what would
Have been a blood bath.

Now home and no longer a "Boy" but a man,
(They had to grow up fast at that time)
And as I gaze at us from that old black and white photo
From so long, long ago,
I see youth eager to get on with a life that had
Been so cruelly interrupted.

So many memories come flooding in.
How I envy the young girl I was, so confident,
In the glow of love.
Just for a moment to feel the intensity
Of that summer day.
Thank you Mama for taking that picture,
To preserve the memory of that place in time.

A DEMAIN (TILL WE MEET AGAIN)

They are old and frail and walk in a measured step,
Their gnarled hands holding fast.
Oh how I envy them.
But we did have over 62 years together.
The sun did shine on us.
Now I fervently strive for the Discipline of Gratitude.

Maybe five more years I ponder.
Just one more exotic trip.
We did have 36 years of seeing the world.
We did have magic times together.
The sun did shine on us.
Oh how desperately I need the Discipline of Gratitude.

Longing for his physical presence,
Pictures of the past,
Letters from long, long ago,
Remembered moments so precious.
The sun did shine on us.
Let me allow myself the Discipline of Gratitude.

Children, Grandchildren, Great Grandchildren,
My home, my family, my friends, my independence,
Let me be struck like an epiphany.
Let me remember all the sacred treasured space.
Let me discipline myself to realize how truly blessed I am.

As the sun inevitably sets,
Let me slip my gnarled hand from yours,
And finally wave a last goodbye.

A House Full of Memories

Pictures, pictures, pictures,
On the coffee table,
On the kitchen table,
On the counter,
The refrigerator, microwave oven.

A virtual soothing rainbow of
Dear faces.
Faces never to be forgotten.
An arc from earliest years,
To late in life.
Old black and white taken over 70 years ago.
Others vibrant color taken recently.

Why so you may ask.
It's a many layered answer.
First and foremost a help on my
Arduous path ahead,
To sit and reflect on the many,
Beautiful scenes depicted.
Memories of love,
Memories of fun,
Memories of adventures.

They shove away the loneliness.
A reminder of how much joy
I've had in a long life.
Seemingly to come alive,
To speak to me,
To remind me where I've been,
What was happening when the
Picture was snapped.
A time machine,
That I can return to,

Be there again, in that moment.
Pictures assure me that it happened.
Makes my loved ones never out of sigh.
Never to be forgotten.

Visit the elderly and you,
Will find that soothing
Rainbow of dear faces easing them thru,
The lonely time.

A Lifetime of Waiting

From earliest childhood, we wait,
To be fed, diaper changed, cuddled.
Later in school,
Waiting for the freedom of summer.
As a pre-teen waiting for that magic number 16,
When it finally comes, ah so sweet, sweet 16.
Waiting for the soldier's safe return from war.
Waiting for the elegant ring for the 3rd finger of the left hand.
Waiting to be a bride.
Ah, the nine months waiting for the blessed event,
Then, waiting to see the children thru to 18.
Now off to college, and waiting to see if all you taught them
paid off.
Waiting to see their success in career, in their mate.
Waiting in the background to be there for the misadventures,
And so hoping not to be needed.
The pleasure of waiting for a trip to far off places,
Half the fun is in the anticipation.
Waiting for an illness to be over, or at times for closure.
Waiting for peace and quiet when there is chaos.
It seems we spend a lifetime of waiting for someone or
something.
And when the waiting has finally ended, it just begins all over
again.
As in the tale of Evangeline, waiting a lifetime to find her
beloved,
Sadly finding him too late.
And when life has ended, from birth to death, the waiting game
is finally over.

A Man for all Seasons

You sit at your desk in your office,
Guiding your employees.
Hurry home for a quick dinner,
Then it's off you go to another desk,
Guiding your students.

I eagerly await your return,
Sitting by the window till 10:00 pm,
Watching the cars go by.
Then, a car turns onto our street,
Its headlights beam like a light house,
Guiding you home to me.

It's been a long day from 7:00-10:00,
And I gleefully acknowledge your return.
We slowly climb the steps to our Sanctuary,
You finally at rest, the long day over.
And on occasion you replay your recorded lecture,
Which as you so often jest,
Is the best sleeping pill around!

A Time Ago

I constantly find myself stealing back,
Back to that other time,
A time decades and decades ago.

Whenever I enter my home I return to a connection,
A secretive archive of memory that my home holds,
A return to echoes that had gone on within its walls.

My personal landscape, it's always there.
I carry it with me, it pleases me.
The imprint and impression of my love
Who lived here never leaves.

A memory is a sanctuary that I can never lose,
In the ghost of loss my love gives me,
An invisible cloak of protection.

A Very Special Trip

July 1987,
Hungary, Poland, Czechoslovakia,
Ah, Prague,
A city of gorgeous architecture.
Each building a work of art,
A city of beauty and tragedy.
Heartbreaking children's drawings from Terezen,
In a museum of the Shoah,
The ancient 12th century Alta Newa Synagogue reeks of
antiquity.
Also a unique synagogue with Hebrew numbers,
On its clock tower.

Colorful Lilliputian homes where Franz Kafka once lived
Walking the Charles Bridge,
The sun winking at us, drying the dewy faces of
Magnificent statuary lining the bridge,
The bridge that spans the tranquil Molda River,
Smetina's home, now a museum, his enchanting music,
Fill our ears.

Dvork's home, now a museum,
Strains of the Largo, from his News World Symphony bring,
Poignant memories of my Father's funeral.
Cab rides,
Metro rides, helpful people.
Municipal Prague Museum: On display, a perfect replica
Of the city in miniature.
When the natural darkness of evening pulls its shades as we,
Traverse the Charles Bridge,
To the end.

Cozily, tucked under, its fragrant aromas precede us as we
Enter the quaint Three Ostrich Restaurant,

Caviar, house wines, chicken soup of potato and eggs,
Fried dumplings, duck and cabbage.
Mouse of ginger and fruits,
All new tastes to an American palate,
Prague, exhales memories of a time gone by.

An Ode to Sabine

Sabine, so adorable, so full of delightful dimples,
So animated, so ready to take on the world.
Ah, to kiss and hug and love you, precious Baby.
You come from a brilliant tapestry,
A tapestry of diversity.
A grandfather of the West, American,
His legacy, Lithuania and Great Britain.
A grandfather from the East, Malaysian,
His legacy, India.
A grandmother of the West, American,
Her legacy, Russia and Poland.
A grandmother of the East, Malaysian,
Her legacy, China.
You are Heinz 57!
You are a United Nations Child.
You are the hope of the future
Your mother, American,
Your father, Malaysian.
Once a seminary student was your Eastern
Grandfather.
A Rabbi your Western
Great Grand Uncle.
Colors and Religions blending together in you peacefully.
Can we see a world of colors and religions do this?
Can we see a world emulate your beautiful family?
You fill your great grandmother's heart with joy,
Knowing that you will carry your
Great Grandfather's Hebrew Name
Moshe
The feminine: Miriam.
Miriam, sister of Moses who watched over him in the river,
Miriam, of the well, supplying water in the desert,

Miriam of the beautiful voice who sand from the
Song of the Sea
Miriam: Life giving force of Water,
Soul touching music.

D Day: 70th Anniversary

After five years and more of devastation
The world wide,
Catastrophic bombings, invasions, battles,
Land and sea and air,
And finally the day arrives,
June 6th, D Day.
To be remembered as the day
When at last we can
Get a peek of a future.
A future of life not death.
A future of building , not destroying.
A future of education for our children.
Not the fear for a life of a
Soldier, sailor, or marine.
Parents can now hope in months,
Not in years
For their returning sons.
Wives can now foresee their returning
Husbands.
It will be 11 months more
To rid the menace in Europe.
It will be called VE Day.
Another 3 more months to finally see VJ Day,
The end of the war in the Pacific.
And the promise of D Day finally
Come true.
The music will be of Homecoming,
Not of loss.
Seventy years have passed since
Than momentous Day of Sacrifice.

Getting A Marriage License ??????????

Spring of 1944, we meet and he leaves to go to war.
Late 1945 he returns, war is over.
1946-1949 we "go together" while he completes
his college degrees.

At long last wedding plans, all set and in place for
Sunday June 12, 1949.
Off we go to City Hall for our marriage license,
Told we can be married on Monday June 13th!!
What, Why?
Because in Massachusetts marriage can only take place,
10 days, excluding Saturdays and Sundays,
after receiving the license,
That's The Law!!

Oh boy, my fiancé says, did we goof this one!
However, we're informed:
We can waive the Law if it's for a good reason, and,
I think you have one.
Great, we respond.
By the way young lady, are you 21?
No, not till Monday June 13th.

Well, we're again at an impasse because I'm legally not 21,
But, but what about our wedding date?
In that case you'll have to get your Fathers' permission.
We can't believe this.
We who have been going together since 1944!!
Sorry,
Off we go to my Dad's factory,
"What's up?" he offers.
Daddy, you won't believe this story,
After hearing our tale of woe and the irony in it,
Off the three of us go, back to City Hall where

Dad gives his permission.
Oh by the way, we're informed, that will cost you double
because of the waiver,
$4.00 instead of $2.00,
My fiancé's remark:
I'm sure this is a sign of things to come:
She'll be an expensive wife!!

Holding On, Yet Going Forward

They stand there together,
Newly wed,
Each holding on to the end of a satin cord,
A satin cord of marriage.
Occasionally, there is a tug,
An argument,
The cord begins to fray.
Tensions build, and it snaps,
Yet, like all strong marriages,
They tie the ends together,
Re-knot their love for each other.
The knot is strong, stronger than the original.
The cord now shorter between them,
The couple closer together.
Through the years, their very tensions,
Will bring them ever closer.
No light can ever pass between them,
They are truly one.

Marriage: A Puzzle, An Analogy

The pieces of the puzzle lay on the table.
I began putting two perfect pieces together.
The edges are smooth, straight and true.
And the picture comes out perfect.
So lovely, so like a fairy tale.
Yet, one little jar, one little eruption and everything falls apart.
The perfect pieces cannot sustain, cannot stay together.
I clear the table of this fantasy.

I put together two pieces.
Not smooth and straight are these,
But jarring and jutting – imperfect.
Yet, they interlock and their very imperfection makes for
strength.
Strength to withstand anything, to keep the
Picture in tact.
No jarring, no eruptions can separate them.
This is what makes a marriage.
This is what marriage is all about.
The imperfect made perfect, a blending.
Till death do we part we said.
Death did come to claim my beloved.
Now I am left alone, with those jutting and
Jarring raw edges.
Left alone bereft of my other half.
Left alone with my imperfection.

MORNING

It was a late October morning,
The air in my bedroom so cold.
Quickly donning slippers and robe,
I pull the vertical flowered print blinds,
And they pop open.

Light floods the room giving a
Natural warmth.
I look out on a new day, only hours old.
This is really a precious gift,
A whole new day ahead to do with it,
Whatever I choose.
The freedom of the open road,
Or delightful confinement of a class.
Maybe just to enjoy getting the house in order,
Or reading a great book.

It's all mine, 24 hours, a gift.
Looking out the window,
The trees all dressed for autumn,
In their delightful colors of red, saffron, and orange.
The ubiquitous squirrels, tails high like a furry sail,
Run playfully over the grass, powdered with frost,
In search of food and hiding places to store,
Their winter supply.
Rabbits too make their appearance,
Standing like silent statues.
Huge black birds, flying in droves,
Piercing the quiet morning with their shrill conversation,
Like haggling old women in noisy gossip.

Looking up, I observe the azure sky, clear and crisp.
Then a streak of white that trails a jet,
The plane, so high it is hidden from sight.

I am reminded of the many times I have been up there,
Streaking through the vast space, heading to a
Wondrous adventure.
But then I think, I really don't have to be in a jet plane,
For adventure,
Every new day has its share, and it starts when,
Those verticals flip open.

NIGHT SHADOWS

When night casts its soft shadows,
And floods my bedroom, sublime,
It reveals years and years of memories,
Together in so many different bedrooms.

Glamorous hotels, as in Caan, France,
Facing the undulating Mediterranean Sea,
The majestic yachts,
Gracefully gliding through the halcyon blue water.

Simple motels,
Off a busy highway,
Just a quick overnight,
On our way to "Somewhere".

Large boats the size of a small city,
The huge waves lapping against its sides,
A land white with ice,
As we anticipate arriving in Alaska.

Small boats on the Nile,
The Nile so narrow,
We feel we can reach out,
And touch the land.

When on a leisurely trip, B and B's to enjoy,
Our bedroom always graced with aromatic linens,
Teas, cakes, chocolates, set on beautiful china,
To indulge our sweet tooth.

But most of all family visits,
No matter how elaborate or small,
Aunts, Uncles and Cousins,
Just being together, made it all worthwhile.

Selma Wolkow

Author, Poet

Love, Loss and Remembrance: A Poetry Anthology

Heirlooms Matter: They Have a Story to Tell

sw1949@gmail.com

ng our bedroom thru the years,
so exquisite, and now so missed,
dows of the past and dreams,
ecome my only companions.

Not an Ordinary Day

No clouds, the sky above seemed
Painted in the blue chloroform of cold.
The sun a golden orb.
Mom in the kitchen,
Breakfast ready,
Six year old son left for school,
Twelve year old daughter upstairs,
Home with the sniffles.
Suddenly from upstairs: Mom, Mom,
Put on the TV, unbelievable words sprouted forth,
We just hear,
The President was shot.
Shock saves in the house,
Shock waves across the country,
Shock waves around the world!
A weekend from hell,
Glued to the TV,
President dies!
Assailant shot to death on TV,
Friday November 22, 1963,
As it was on December 7, 1941
Another Day of Infamy.

NOT YET, NOT YET

Why does my heart go on beating?
It is broken beyond repair!
I so long to be with you my beloved,
But his answer is always: not yet, not yet.

My time will come, that is a certainty,
For I guess I have more to do,
And thru it all I must bear the pain,
Bare the everlasting longing,
For his answer is still: not yet, not yet.

I have been so fortunate,
I have known the elixir of love,
We shared over 62 wondrous years,

But oh, I am so tired,
So emotionally tired,
Of hearing: not yet, not yet.

I beg for the bliss of not feeling,
No longer longing for what cannot be,
Living only in my precious memories,
Until at last my soul mate,
Finally says: Yes

Reflections

"Will it be just two?" asked the waiter.
"Ah yes," Helen and I plaintively replied.
Ensconced in the booth, our thoughts reflect our loss.
"We used to be four," Helen murmured,
"We used to have such good times together,"
I echoed.

Everything seems to start with we used to.
We're in a different place now.
Our cup is half full, half of us is gone.
Oh how we long for the camaraderie we had,
The trips,
The films,
The restaurants,
The theater,
We used to be four.

4

Remembering

I sit outdoors,
Comfortable in my old age,
Comfortable with my white hair,
Comfortable with my wrinkled skin,
As the sun begins its magical descent.

Then in the velvet darkness of night,
Memories come cascading down around me,
Like sparks, like fireflies, like falling stars,
And I see the young girl I was.

Frolicking with her guy at the seaside,
The air pungent and fresh and salty,
The beloved guy who will become her husband.
I see them strolling hand in hand,
Thru the crackling leaves.

On an autumn day,
Above the sky an azure blue,
The air a fragrant fall perfume.
I see them huddled together on a snowy night,
The air so cold, it hurts to breath,
Rushing off to see a film.

Or meeting friends for a party,
So full of energy, vitality and love.
It's a mild spring day in May,
It will become memorable,
Because, because it will be the first day,
Of the rest of their lives.

Like the warmth of the day,
She will be enfolded in the warmth of his love,

A love they will share for the next 62 ½ years.

Sometimes

Sometimes, as I lay in bed
I pretend,
Pretend I am in your arms,
My head resting,
On your shoulder
As we watch our favorite TV programs.

Sometimes, we lay in bed,
Like a pair of spoons.
Sometimes, as I lay in bed,
I pretend,
Pretend I annoy you as my toes tickle your legs.
Sometimes, I can almost see the door open from the bathroom,
And your return to bed.
Sometimes, as I lay in bed,
I pretend,
Pretend I can feel the bounce in the bed.
As you put on
Your socks and shoes
Getting dressed for work.
And after retired making breakfast and calling me from the
kitchen,
"Breakfast is Reaaaady"
Sometimes as I lay in bed.
I pretend,
Pretend I can just reach out and touch you,
Sometimes, sometimes,
I lay on your pillow,
Sodden with real tears that pour from eyes,
That will forever long to see you.

Sparks Fly On Thanksgiving Day

Angie from Columbia, South America,
Angie 23, vivacious and so sweet
Aha, Angie for Eric? Maybe.
Ronni and Norm's closest friends' son
Eric, so shy, at 33 still searching for that special girl,
Maybe she could bring out the best in him.

So onto the computer, Face Book here we come.
They meet, exchange pictures and information.
Unbelievably, a few days later,
Eric drives from Maryland to Pennsylvania
To meet Angie in person.

Yes, she sure did bring out his best, Shy? Who said that!
Yes, they hit if off and lo and behold they enter in the New Year,
Together in Times Square, New York,
Together on the Brooklyn Bridge,
They employ an old Parisian tradition,
Carving their initials on a padlock,
Throwing the key into the river.

It's miraculous, two distant souls found each other,
It's like a Hollywood movie,
But this is real.
They are like one,
In touch every day.

How can this happen so quickly, you might ask?
Affairs of the heart are completely unpredictable,
Sometimes, when its right,
Couples just know it almost immediately.
And so we observe them: Angie and Eric,
Waiting for the next step,

Wishing them joy,
Flash: Update,
Phones ringing,
Face Book comes alive,
Eric asks Angie to marry him!
Angie says yes!
Wedding in May!

The Old Clock

I am Ilias Ingraham, a wood clock.
I have a round face with Roman numeral numbers.
Beneath my face are chimes.
On May 30, 1871, I was a wedding gift.
No issue came from this marriage,
However, a great devotion grew and grew.

This couple lived near Rose Brown,,
A warm and loving woman with 6 children.
When the wife became old and ill Rose was there
To comfort and provide food.
The now aged husband, ever so grateful after losing his beloved,
to show appreciation gave me to Rose.
I became part of the family.
Roses' husband Jacob wound my charms each evening.

I chimed in the morning to wake the family,
I chimed when it was dinner time,
I chimed when it was bed time for the children,
My melodic voice filled their modest home.

When Roses' family had grown and left,
Frances, her sister-in-law admired me and the ever,
So generous Rose quickly responded, I'll let you have it.

Now I chimed for the Massick family until I
Was no longer needed and I was disposed to the attic.
It was such a lonely and sad time for me.
Many years passed until one day Frances' niece Esther,
Was visiting.
Quite suddenly Frances said to her niece,
I have your Mothers clock, and I think you should take it.
Take it I will, but I'll give it to my daughter Selma.

Thus it was that I became part of a new family,
My chimes long silent were repaired.
My melodic voice once again filled a home with joy.

Roses' Granddaughter Selma will eventually pass me
On to one of her many Grandchildren or Great Grandchildren.
So after 142 years I can still look forward,
To someday chiming for another young family.

The Permission Slip

The plain ordinary pine rests there.
The plain ordinary paper lies atop,
The plain ordinary pen reposes astride,
The plain ordinary tears overflow,
I can no long see thru the waterfall.

He bids me pick up the pen,
He bids me write upon the paper,
He bids me feel the pine as a support as I write,
But can I do it?
Can I possibly put pen to paper?

Give myself permission to do what?
To go alone where we had been together,
No longer able to share an experience that we had shared,
The pen remains in my hand,
The paper still unused: perhaps, someday_____.

The Telephone Ring Prevails

The telephone awakens me from my sleep,
Just one ring,
Sometimes it's shrill as a screeching tire,
Sometimes a muffled echo in a cave,
Sometimes, soft as a summer breeze,
What is it? How is it? Why is it?
The telephone ring prevails.

I welcome it, a sign?
Perchance a message?
It started as soon as you passed,
It continues resonating only inside my head,
What is it? How is it? Why is it?
The telephone ring prevails.

Someday I'll surely find the answer,
The meaning of those solitary rings,
For now I wait, deep in slumber,
In the bed we shared so many years together,
It was our island in the vast sea,
It was our oasis in the searing desert
The telephone ring prevails.

Thoughts on Seventy Years Together

At the beginning,
Nineteen hundred and forty-four,
A meeting in May,
Sweethearts,
Tender young love
Under a starlit sky,
A fiancé, love starting to mature,
An engagement,
And as stars have a natural gravity to each other,
So too us, a wedding,
Our gravity forever,
A husband, a wife, loving and enjoying almost sixty years,
Parenthood,
And as it began, inevitably, so must it end, loss would come,
Now a widow,
Yet our two stars never lose their gravity,
The pull remains,
Twinkling to each other for eternity.
Sweetheart, Fiancé, Wife, Mother, Widow

Waiting at the Window

Waiting at the window on a cold evening for your return,
I know you let the class out at nine and it's almost
nine forty-five.
And then I see the hood of the car round the street,
The air becomes perfumed and I seem to inhale in my lungs,
Pure unadulterated joy.

It's a lovely summer early evening,
I hear "Daddy is home" and I see you framed in the doorway,
And as you bend over to kiss the kids your eyes lock with mine,
I experience pure unadulterated joy.

These feelings are as fleeting
As a blink of an eye,
Yet, weeks and months and years
Are layered and become a foundation,
The bedrock of our marriage.

What Really Matters: Being Alone Together

The film was so exciting,
The party was a howling success,
The opera was truly magnificent,
The symphony was resounding and memorable,
The trip a beautiful and impressive experience,
The courses enriched our minds.

Yet nothing, nothing could ever compare to our home,
Wherever it was, no matter how humble or grand,
Returning to it was always, always,
Entering our very special enchanted, land.

What Were Your Thoughts

Just 18 years old
Boarding the troop ship
Heavy pack on your back
The ship the Queen Elizabeth
So fast was she
No convoy was needed
She could outrun any sub
What were your thoughts?
You wrote "What's a little bullet wound?"
You wrote "What's a little shrapnel wound?"
You wrote "I'll make it back"
But what were your thoughts deep down?
At 18 you were not vulnerable
At 18 nothing could get you
You wrote "I'll see you again"
You wrote "We had such little time together"
You wrote "It just can't end now"
But what were your thoughts deep, deep down?
You did come home,
You did make it thru the dangerous journey
And I never thought to ask
Somehow finally safe at home it never came up.
And now, as I ponder so many, many years later
I can never know the answer.
You are gone.
And would you really have told me you were scared?
Would you have told me that it might end
On a lonely battlefield in the cold, cold foxhole?
And after all, does it really matter now?